Interjections

by Ann Heinrichs

Content Adviser: Kathy Rzany, M.A., Adjunct Professor,
School of Education, Dominican University, River Forest, Illinois

Published by The Child's World®
1980 Lookout Drive • Mankato, MN 56003-1705
800-599-READ • www.childsworld.com

Cover and page 1: Serhiy Kobyakov/Shutterstock.com; 5: Sergey Novikov/Shutterstock.com; 7: Esteban De Armas/Shutterstock.com; 9: KK Tan/Shutterstock.com; 10: namatae/Shutterstock.com; 13: Danie Nel Photography/Shutterstock.com; 15: Monkey Business Images/Shutterstock.com; 16: AFH/Shutterstock.com; 18: Kamira/Shutterstock.com; 20: antoniodiaz/Shutterstock.com; 22: Aaron Amat/Shutterstock.com; 23: Alter-ego/Shutterstock.com; 24: medesulda/Shutterstock.com; 25: Tukaram.Karve/Shutterstock.com; 27: Christian Bertrand/Shutterstock.com; 29: Bart Lapeere/Shutterstock.com

ISBN: 9781503832428
LCCN: 2018957533

Printed in the United States of America
PA02423

ABOUT THE AUTHOR

Ann Heinrichs is the author of more than 200 books for children and young adults. She has also enjoyed successful careers as a children's book editor and an advertising copywriter. Ann grew up in Fort Smith, Arkansas, and now lives in Chicago, Illinois.

Contents

CHAPTER ONE

What Is an Interjection?

[**Definition: An interjection is a word used to get attention or express a feeling.**]

EXAMPLES

Wow! Yahoo! Ouch! Yuck! Yum!

Guess what all these words are? They're interjections! Can you imagine life without them? You'd have lots of trouble saying how you feel. Interjections are words you use to get attention or express feelings.

Some interjections express happiness, sadness, or surprise.

EXAMPLES

Yippee! It's party time!
Alas, the library is closed today.
Eek! There's a mouse under my chair!

These kids are yelling a big, loud interjection. What do you suppose that interjection is?

Some interjections are cheers.

EXAMPLES

Hurray! We finally won after all these years!

Bravo! You did a great job!

Some interjections are greetings or goodbyes.

EXAMPLES

Hi, Sarah. How's your hamster?

So long, Bart.

And some interjections just sort of fill up space!

EXAMPLES

We only have, um, 50 videos.

Well, make sure you get some more.

Some experts say interjections are the earliest form of human speech. Imagine cavemen or prehistoric hunters. They might have spoken to each other in grunts and shouts. They might have said things that meant **Hey!** or **Whoopee!** or **Wow!**

Our communication has developed much more since then, but we still need lots of interjections. Let's check it out!

DID YOU KNOW?

The word *interjection* comes from two Latin words—*inter* ("between") and *jactus* ("thrown"). So an interjection is a word "thrown between" other words.

Early hunters probably used interjections to communicate with one another while hunting.

CHAPTER TWO

Words That Stand Alone

Rule: Interjections are not related to any other part of a sentence.

Interjections don't modify, or describe, anything, as adjectives and adverbs do. They don't name anything, as nouns and pronouns do. They're not action words, as verbs are. And they don't join words together, as prepositions and conjunctions do. They just stand alone.

When speaking, it's easy to make an interjection stand alone. Often you just say the interjection and stop. Sometimes you naturally make a little pause in your voice before going on.

What about when you're writing interjections? You still need to make the interjection stand alone. You need to show what your voice would be doing if you were speaking. You do that with punctuation marks.

Rule: Strong interjections are followed by an exclamation point. Mild interjections are set off by commas.

You can often spot an interjection. It's followed by an exclamation point (!). The exclamation point comes after strong interjections—those that express strong feelings. Maybe you're excited. Maybe you're even yelling!

EXAMPLES

Oops! My monkey jumped off its perch.

Hey! Get that monkey off my head!

Yoo-hoo! Come back here, Frisky.

"Hey! I see Frisky hiding in that tree." The strong interjection **Hey!** uses an exclamation point to express strong feelings or excitement.

There are no bananas for this little fellow today. If he could talk, he might use the strong interjection **Darn!** or the mild interjection **Gee.**

Some interjections are calmer and quieter. They're called mild interjections. To make mild interjections stand alone, use commas (,).

EXAMPLES

Say, **do you have any bananas for my monkey?**

No, **we have no bananas today.**

Well, **when will you have bananas?**

Gee, **I really don't know.**

CHAPTER THREE

Wait! Stop! It's a Verb!

EXAMPLES

Stop! Look! Help!

Wait! Stay!

All these words have exclamation points. They're spoken with strong feelings, and they stand alone. They're words you might call out or even yell at the top of your voice. But watch out! They're not interjections. They're really verbs.

Rule: An exclamation point follows any kind of exclamation. Exclamations are things you exclaim, or say with strong feelings.

Exclamation points are good clues for finding interjections. However, not every exclamation point means you have an interjection. Exclamation points follow any kind of exclamation. Exclamations are things you exclaim, or call out with strong feelings such as excitement or surprise.

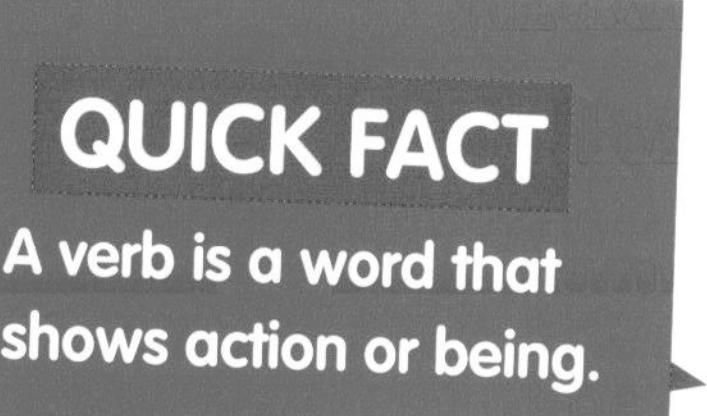

Each word in the example box on page 11 is an action word. **Stop** is an action. So are **look, help, wait,** and **stay.** These words all describe things to do or ways to be. Therefore, they are verbs.

Definition: A sentence is a group of words that expresses a complete thought and ends with a period or exclamation point. Every sentence has a subject and a verb.

Wait! There's more. **Stop!** and **Look!** and the other examples are also complete sentences. All sentences have a subject and a verb. We know where the verb is. But where is the subject?

The subject is **you.** We don't see or say the word **you.** However, **you** is understood when commands are given. **Stop!** and **Look!** are commands. If someone says **Stop!** to you, you know it means **You stop!**

She's saying **Stop!** There's no doubt about it—she means **You stop!**

CHAPTER FOUR

Happy Interjections

Surprise, delight, and other happy feelings are perfect reasons to use interjections. Suppose you just found out you won 100 free pizzas. Which of these interjections would you use?

EXAMPLES

Wow! Gosh! Golly! Gee whiz! Yeow! Yowie! My goodness! Oh boy!

When your friends found out about the pizzas, they might break into cheers:

EXAMPLES

Hurray! Yay! Yahoo! Yippee! Whoopee! Right on!

When you eat the pizzas, your interjections might be **Yum!** or **Yummy!** or **Mmm!**

If you're trying to get someone's attention, you say **Hey!** or maybe **Yoo-hoo!** Greetings and goodbyes have interjections too—**hi, hello, goodbye, bye,** and **so long.**

DID YOU KNOW?

In a way, **goodbye** is a whole sentence. It's a short form of the old English farewell, "God be with you."

Ha! can mean "Oh boy!" or "See there!" or "I don't believe that." If you came up with a great idea, you'd say **Aha!** But if you're laughing, you say **Ha ha!** And don't forget Santa!

EXAMPLE

Merry Christmas! Ho ho ho!

What interjection do you think these teammates are yelling?

CHAPTER FIVE

Not-So-Happy Interjections

Many interjections are things you say when you're not so happy. Maybe you're shocked or disappointed. Maybe you're annoyed. Maybe you're just plain sad. Whatever your feelings are, there's an interjection to help you express them.

This little boy is feeling sad. He might be thinking of interjections such as **Oh dear** or **Darn.**

Suppose you did your homework, but the dog ate it. Which of these interjections would you use?

EXAMPLES

Nuts! Darn! Shoot! Oh dear! Alas!

If you're scared, displeased, or just fed up, there are plenty of interjections for you!

EXAMPLES

Eek! I saw a snake in the grass.

Yikes! There's a whole nest of ants!

Yuck! Some broccoli just landed in my ice cream!

Ouch! That mosquito bit my leg!

Uh-oh! Sparky turned the garbage can over again.

Good grief! He's been running in circles for an hour.

If something is annoying you, you have a choice of interjections. **Scram!** means "Go away!" To make a flying insect go away, you wave your hands in the air and say **Shoo!** One interjection is just for cats—**Scat!**

What if someone says your kitty is afraid of mice? You might say **Not!** But if you say "No way!" they might say **Way!**

Suppose there was a big announcement on the news: "Scientists have discovered that chickens lay eggs."

There's only one interjection for this situation: **Duh!**

CHAPTER SIX

Ways to Fill Up Space

Some interjections seem to have no purpose. They just seem to fill up space. But they can be very helpful in conversation. For example, interjections can "get you going" when you start to say something.

EXAMPLES

Gee, I'm getting really tired.
So, you think you've had enough?
Oh, I thought it was time to go.
Well, try not to be late next time.
Say, where did you put that lizard?
Boy, that was a loud noise.

Sometimes when you're talking, you need to stop and think a second. Interjections fill that gap while you're thinking.

EXAMPLES

We should be done by, uh, three o'clock.
I wonder where Tigger is. Hmm. Maybe he's on the roof.
The last time I saw him was, um, Thursday.

CHAPTER SEVEN

Interjections with No Words

Some interjections are just sounds. Some of them seem to explode right out of your mouth! These sounds are not words. Many of the sounds don't even exist in regular spoken English. So how can they be written down? We use certain groups of letters to stand for mouth and throat sounds.

Some interjections are just sounds. When you want someone to be quiet, you say **Sh!**

Did you ever clear your throat to get someone's attention? That throat-clearing sound is spelled **Ahem!** What do you say when you want someone to be quiet? You blow air past your tongue to say **Sh!** Did you ever hear a joke and start giggling? That giggling sound is spelled **hee-hee.**

DID YOU KNOW?

The clicking sound is a regular part of speech in some African languages. They're sometimes called click languages. Speakers of these languages include the Zulu, Xhosa, San, and Khoikhoi people of southern Africa.

Tsk-tsk stands for a clicking sound. It's made by clicking the tip of your tongue against the back of your teeth. It means "That's too bad" or "Shame on you!"

EXAMPLES

Tsk-tsk! That's a terrible bruise.

Tsk-tsk! You've spilled paint all over the floor.

Suppose you want to say, "Hey—over here!" very quietly. You use your lips and tongue to say **Pss!** or **Psst!**

What if you narrowly escape a disaster? You blow air through your lips to say **Whew!** Another great interjection is **Ugh!** It's a grunt or groan way in the back of your mouth, near your throat.

EXAMPLES

Psst! I'm under the bed.
Whew! That weasel almost bit my leg.
Ugh! This baloney sandwich is moldy!

CHAPTER EIGHT

Bang! Zap! Pow!

Comics and cartoons are full of great interjections. Some are real words, but others just stand for sounds. They all add energy and excitement to the action. They help you hear what's happening, besides seeing it.

Zoom! and **Whoosh!** are the sounds of things flying through the air. When something lands on a hard surface, it might go **Wham!** or **Whap!** If it's wet, it goes **Splat!** Explosions might go **Boom!** or **Kaboom!** or **Kablooey!**

Lots of human sounds show up in comics too. Pirates and sailors seem to love saying **Argh!** It's more like a growl than a word. When people bump into things, they go **Oof!** or **Unh!**

When this juice hits the floor, you might describe the sound as **Splat!**

Can you tell what's happening when you see this comic-book interjection? The interjection **Wham!** also helps you hear what's happening.

Zzzzz stands for the sound of snoring. Have you ever heard someone say they're going to "catch some z's"? It means they're going to get some sleep!

Can you think of any other comic or cartoon interjections? Do you have some favorites?

CHAPTER NINE

Interjections around the World

No matter where in the world you live, you need interjections. It's fun to learn about interjections in other languages. Take a look at the examples on the next page. You'll see that many foreign-language interjections are very similar to English interjections.

DID YOU KNOW?

In Spanish, interjections and other exclamations get special punctuation marks. An upside-down exclamation point (¡) comes at the beginning, and a regular exclamation point comes at the end.

These girls from India use interjections just like you do.

SPANISH	PRONUNCIATION	MEANING
¡He! or ¡Eh!	eh	Hey!
¡Ay!	eye	Alas!
¡Oh!	oh	Oh!
¡Olé!	oh-LAY	Bravo!
FRENCH		
Zut!	zoot	Shoot! or Darn!
Hé!	eh	Hey! or Well!
Aïe!	eye	Ouch! or Oh dear!
Ouf!	oof	Whew!
GERMAN		
He! or Hei!	heh or hi	Hey!
Au!	ow	Oh! or Ouch!
Ach!	ahk	Alas!

In the United States, some regions and culture groups have their own interjections. In some places, **eh** is used in asking questions. **Yo** is an all-purpose exclamation. It often means **hi** or **hey.**

EXAMPLES

Tired of practicing, eh?

Yo, Jesse. What's up?

Are there any special interjections in the area where you live?

Kids around the world, such as these boys from Spain, use lots of interjections when they're playing. They need to express excitement, joy, disappointment, and plenty of other feelings.

CHAPTER TEN

Do Animals Have Interjections?

Animals can't speak in words. They can only make sounds. Like humans, they express surprise, joy, sadness, and many other feelings. So you might say they "speak" in interjections!

People have figured out ways to spell animal sounds. Some are **bowwow, meow, quack, honk, moo, oink, cluck-cluck, cock-a-doodle-doo, grr,** and **hee-haw.** Can you think of any others?

How can you tell what an animal means? Often you can't tell.

DID YOU KNOW?

BARKING AROUND THE WORLD

Other languages have their own ways of spelling animal sounds. In Japan, a barking dog says *wan, wan!* ("wahn, wahn"). In Ghana, it says *wahu, wahu!* ("WAH-hoo, WAH-hoo"). In Germany, it's *wau, wau!* ("wow, wow"). In Turkey, it's *hav, hav!* ("how, how").

But if you know the animal well, you might be able to figure it out. **Bowwow!** could mean, "I'm happy to see you!" **Meow!** could mean, "I don't like that new cat food!"

Do you have a pet? Or do you know another animal well? Can you tell what some of its sounds mean?

Quack! What is this duck trying to say? Perhaps he's saying, "I'm hungry!" or "Feed me!" or "Where's the lake?"

Fun with Interjections

Here are some fun exercises. Write down your answers on a separate piece of paper.

1. Fill in the blanks with an interjection.

   a. _________ ! What a game!

   b. _________ , I wish the movie would start.

   c. Can you pick us up by, _________ , five o'clock?

   d. _________ ! I forgot to study for the quiz.

   e. _________ , Sarah. Do you want to hang out later?

2. What are these interjections used for?

   a. boom!

   b. zzzzz!

   c. ahem!

   d. ouch!

   e. psst!

See page 32 for the answers. Don't peek!

How to Learn More

IN THE LIBRARY

Bailer, Darice, and Kelsey Oseid (illustrator). *Iris and Ian Learn about Interjections.* Chicago, IL: Norwood House Press, 2015.

Cleary, Brian P., and Brian Gable (illustrator). *Cool! Whoa! Ah and Oh! What Is an Interjection?* Minneapolis, MN: Millbrook Press, 2014.

Lehrhaupt, Adam, and Jared Chapman (illustrator). *Wordplay.* New York, NY: Arthur A. Levine, 2017.

Meister, Cari, and Holli Conger (illustrator). *Ouch! It Bit Me! A Book about Interjections.* Mankato, MN: Amicus, 2016.

ON THE WEB

Visit our website for links about interjections:
childsworld.com/links

Note to Parents, Teachers, and Librarians: We routinely verify our web links to make sure they are safe and active sites. So encourage your readers to check them out!

Index

Answers

Fun with Interjections

Question 1:
There are many possible answers.
Here are some suggestions:

a. **Wow!** What a game!
b. **Gee,** I wish the movie would start.
c. Can you pick us up by, **um,** five o'clock?
d. **Uh-oh!** I forgot to study for the quiz.
e. **Hey,** Sarah. Do you want to hang out later?

Question 2:
a. an explosion
b. snoring
c. clearing the throat
d. pain
e. getting someone's attention